NEW HOPE
FOR LIFE'S
CHALLENGES

Reflections

——— *on* ———

1 Peter

From the Bible-Teaching Ministry of

Charles R. Swindoll

INSIGHT FOR LIVING

Insight for Living's Bible teacher, Chuck Swindoll, has devoted his life to the clear, practical application of God's Word and His grace. A pastor at heart, Chuck has served as senior pastor to congregations in Texas, Massachusetts, and California. He currently leads Stonebriar Community Church in Frisco, Texas, but Chuck's listening audience extends far beyond a local church body. As a leading program in Christian broadcasting, *Insight for Living* airs in major Christian radio markets, through more than 2,100 outlets worldwide, in 16 languages, and to a growing webcast audience. Chuck's extensive writing ministry has also served the body of Christ worldwide, and his leadership as president and now chancellor of Dallas Theological Seminary has helped prepare and equip a new generation for ministry. Chuck and Cynthia, his partner in life and ministry, have four grown children and ten grandchildren.

Based on the outlines, charts, and transcripts of Charles R. Swindoll's sermons, the Bible study guide text was developed and written by the Pastoral Ministries Department of Insight for Living.

Editor in Chief:
Cynthia Swindoll

Study Guide Writer:
Brian Goins

Senior Editor and Assistant Writer:
Wendy Peterson

Editor and Assistant Writer:
Marla Alupoaicei

Editor:
Amy LaFuria

Typographer:
Bob Haskins

Rights and Permissions:
The Meredith Agency

Unless otherwise identified, all Scripture references are from the New American Standard Bible © The Lockman Foundation 1960, 1962, 1963, 1968, 1971, 1972, 1973, 1975, 1977, 1995. Used by permission. Scripture taken from the Holy Bible, New International Version © 1973, 1978, 1984 by the International Bible Society used by permission of Zondervan Bible Publishers [NIV]. Scripture quotations from THE MESSAGE © 1993, 1994, 1995 by Eugene H. Peterson used by permission of NavPress Publishing Group. Other translations cited are the The New Living Translation [NLT] and the New King James Version [NKJV].

An effort has been made to locate sources and obtain permission where necessary for the quotations used in this book. In the event of any unintentional omission, a modification will gladly be incorporated in future printings.

ISBN 1-57972-441-8
Cover design: Michael Standlee Designs
Cover images: Creatas.com, Thinkstock.com, Michael Standlee
Printed in the United States of America

CONTENTS

INTRODUCTION

When life's struggles strangle your spirit, nothing helps like hope. Hope is as essential to our survival as air or water. Without hope, failures feel final. Marriages fall apart. Dreams fade.

Where can you turn when life's trials sap your strength? Try reading a letter by a seasoned fisherman. Tucked away toward the back of your Bible rests a letter brimming with encouragement for people in hopeless situations. Persecuted by the Romans, ostracized by their neighbors, and beset with "fiery trials," the new converts in the first century needed new hope. The gospel of Jesus Christ shared by a disciple named Simon Peter offered them that hope.

You may be going through a tough time right now. A past mistake may haunt your every thought. Perhaps your marriage is on an unpredictable fault line. Or your coworkers criticize you for obeying the truth. Whatever your burden, the book of 1 Peter will offer you new hope in the midst of trying times in this twenty-first century. Are you ready? Let's join Peter now to find new hope for life's struggles and answers to some of life's toughest questions.

Charles R. Swindoll

Charles R. Swindoll

PUTTING TRUTH
INTO ACTION

Knowledge apart from application falls short of God's desire for His children. He wants us to apply what we learn so that we will change and grow. This Bible study guide was prepared with these goals in mind. As you go through the following pages, we hope your desire to discover biblical truth will grow as your understanding of God's Word increases and that you will be encouraged to apply what you've learned.

To assist you in your study, we've included a section called **Living Insights** at the end of each lesson. These exercises will challenge you to study further and to think of specific ways to put your discoveries into action.

Each Living Insights section is followed by **Small Group Insights**. These thought-provoking questions will help you to facilitate discussion of the important concepts and principles in the chapter and apply them to your life.

There are many ways to use this guide—in personal devotions, group studies, discussions with friends and family, and Sunday school classes. And, of course, it's an ideal study aid when you're listening to its corresponding *Insight for Living* radio series.

To benefit most from this Bible study guide, we encourage you to consider it a spiritual journal. That's why we've included space in the Living Insights for recording your thoughts and discoveries. We hope you'll return to those sections often for review and encouragement as you continue to grow in your walk with Christ.

Insight for Living

NEW HOPE
FOR LIFE'S
CHALLENGES

Reflections

—— *on* ——

1 Peter

Chapter 1

NEW HOPE
BEYOND FAILURE
Selected Scriptures

The Bay of Pigs. Watergate. Whitewater. History rarely glosses over failure, much to the dismay of politicians. But have you ever thought about the fact that the Bible doesn't gloss over people's failures, either?

The biblical drama unfolds with a cast of tainted, fallible, and frankly, quite human characters. Our Scripture heroes and heroines possessed great strengths as well as debilitating weaknesses. Remember the achievements and the anger of Moses? The brute strength and sensuality of Samson? The godliness and guile of Jacob? The blessing and bitterness of Naomi? The wisdom and wantonness of Solomon? Our ancestors in the faith were forced to confront their sinful habits, overcome obstacles, and work through personal failures in order to become all that God had created them to be.

Rarely do we find more of a walking contradiction in terms than in Simon Peter. The "Rock," as Jesus named him, walked on water, yet cowered at the sight of a storm. He publicly proclaimed Jesus as "the Christ, the Son of the living God," but later denied knowing Him. He slashed his sword at hardened soldiers when they came to take Jesus away, but then scurried away in fear after a slave girl recognized him as one of Christ's followers.

Peter's passions and quick tongue often got him into trouble. At times he was astute, at others obtuse. Courageously loyal, yet frequently cowardly. A glowing success . . . and a dismal failure. However, when we turn to 1 Peter 1:1, we don't read, "Peter, the

This chapter has been adapted from "Peter: The Man and His Message," in the Bible study guide *Hope in Hurtful Times*, written by Ken Gire, from the Bible-teaching ministry of Charles R. Swindoll (Anaheim, Calif.: Insight for Living, 1990), pp. 1–11.

man who turned his back on his best friend," or "Peter, the man who denied Christ." We simply read, "Peter, an apostle of Jesus Christ." This tainted, fallible human being found hope beyond grievous failure. He grew to become the Rock, a loyal apostle and follower of Christ.

Peter's Finest Hour

The gospel writer Matthew offers us an intimate portrait of this disciple called Peter. The *Dictionary of Jesus and the Gospels* describes Matthew's writing this way:

> Matthew presents the disciples as a nameless, face-less, collective unity. Peter stands out in sharp relief against this backdrop of anonymity, being the only named disciple to become the focus of special attention. . . . In his strengths and in his weaknesses he can be an example to Matthew's church; so Matthew accentuates the truly human element in Peter. The church would find much in common with Peter's typically human characteristics. In his likeness to ordinary believers with their highs and lows, he provides a means of instructing the church in the path of discipleship.[1]

A poignant illustration of this fact jumps off the page in Matthew 16:13–20. As they walked along the streets of Caesarea Philippi, Jesus gave his disciples a pop quiz:

> Now when Jesus came into the district of Caesarea Philippi, He was asking His disciples, "Who do people say that the Son of Man is?" (Matt. 16:13)

The disciples answered:

> "Some say John the Baptist; and others, Elijah; but still others, Jeremiah, or one of the prophets." (v. 14)

Jesus countered by pointedly asking them:

> "But who do *you* say that I am?" (v. 15, emphasis added)

---

1. *Dictionary of Jesus and the Gospels,* ed. Joel B. Green, Scot McKnight, I. Howard Marshall (Downers Grove, Ill.: InterVarsity Press, 1992), p. 183.

A Startling Confession

Jesus addressed His question to the whole class of disciples. But Simon was the one who immediately piped up like an eager student in the front row:

"You are the Christ, the Son of the living God." (v. 16)

In his single profound statement, Simon affirmed two key theological titles of Jesus: Messiah and Deity. *Christ*, or *Christos* in the Greek, was the New Testament equivalent of *Messiah*. Simon recognized that Jesus was the long-awaited Savior of Israel as well as the God of the universe.

Simon's magnificent declaration echoed back to the prophecy of Jeremiah:

"Behold, the days are coming," declares the Lord,
"When I will raise up for David a righteous Branch;
And He will reign as king and act wisely
And do justice and righteousness in the land. . . .
And this is His name by which He will be called,
'The Lord our righteousness.'" (Jer. 23:5–6)

Though he was familiar with the prophecies concerning Christ, it's doubtful that Simon Peter recognized just how profound his answer was. But the Rock had answered the million-dollar question correctly!

Jesus Blesses Simon

Jesus responded to Simon Peter's confession with a blessing that must have turned the other disciples green with envy:

And Jesus said to him, "Blessed are you, Simon Bar-jona, because flesh and blood did not reveal this to you, but My Father who is in heaven. I also say to you that you are Peter, and upon this rock I will build My church; and the gates of Hades will not overpower it. I will give you the keys of the kingdom of heaven; and whatever you bind on earth shall have been bound in heaven, and whatever you loose on earth shall have been loosed in heaven." (Matt. 16:17–19)

Though Peter was singled out from the disciples, Jesus made it abundantly clear that the correct answer was not derived solely from Peter's gray matter. God the Father had impressed this knowledge and these inspired words upon Peter's heart. After Peter's startling affirmation, Jesus bestowed upon him a strong name: Simon the fisherman became Peter the Rock.[2]

Jesus not only acknowledged Peter's profound answer, He also bestowed a staggering blessing upon him: the "keys of the kingdom of heaven" (Matt. 16:19). Christ delegated to Peter authority over spiritual matters in heaven as well as on earth. Peter was riding high on the crest of Jesus' approval when tragedy struck.

Peter Rebukes Jesus

After He pronounced this blessing on Peter, Jesus warned His disciples not to tell anyone that He was the Christ (Matt. 16:20). As the days leading up to his death dwindled, He began to prepare his closest followers for the difficult upcoming events.

> From that time Jesus began to show His disciples that He must go to Jerusalem, and suffer many things from the elders and chief priests and scribes, and be killed, and be raised up on the third day. Peter took Him aside and began to rebuke Him, saying, "God forbid it, Lord! This shall never happen to you." But He turned and said to Peter, "Get behind me, Satan! You are a stumbling block to Me; for you are not setting your mind on God's interests, but man's." (Matt. 16:21–23)

Peter was clearly appalled at Jesus' references to His impending death. But Christ quickly set Peter straight about the importance of focusing on the things of God rather than on his own ideas about what should happen. Why? Because Jesus knew that His purpose on earth was to submit Himself to the will of the Father and to die in the place of His people. And He knew what Peter's reaction would be when the stakes were raised.

---

2. Jesus uses two Greek words when referring to Simon Peter as the "Rock." He first uses the Greek word *petros*—the singular masculine noun for *rock*. However, when He says, "and upon this rock I will build my church" (Matt. 16:18), He uses the feminine singular noun of *rock*, which means "bedrock" or "large mass of rock." Jesus may have been referring to Peter and all the disciples as the "bedrock" which formed the foundation of the church (Eph. 2:20).

Peter's Darkest Hour

Fast-forward to the Upper Room at the Feast of Unleavened Bread. Jesus' time was short. The chief priests and scribes who were seeking to dispose of this upstart Galilean had finally found their turncoat in Judas Iscariot. Luke 22:3–4 states:

> And Satan entered into Judas who was called Iscariot, belonging to the number of the twelve. And he went away and discussed with the chief priests and officers how he might betray Him to them.

Ultimately, Judas agreed to betray Jesus for thirty silver coins! Peter's darkest hour came on the same tragic night.

A Staggering Confession

The bread was broken and the wine poured. As the disciples ate the bread and drank the wine of the new covenant, Jesus made a shocking proclamation:

> "But behold, the hand of the one betraying Me is with Mine on the table. For indeed, the Son of Man is going as it has been determined; but woe to that man by whom He is betrayed." (Luke 22:21–22)

We know from the earlier context that Satan entered Judas and the deed was done. However, at this point, the other disciples had no clue which of them would betray their Lord. In fact, Luke says, "They began to discuss among themselves which one of them it might be who was going to do this thing" (v. 23). Judas would not have been a likely choice. As the treasurer, he was entrusted with the disciples' money, so he surely possessed a special position of honor and trust among the twelve.

The disciples moved from arguing over treachery to bickering over greatness (v. 24). No doubt Peter's booming voice drowned out the others. But Jesus turned the disciples' argument on its head with a humbling paradox: "The one who is the greatest among you must become like the youngest, and the leader like the servant" (v. 26). Then Jesus singled out Peter from the other disciples.

Jesus Singles Out Simon Peter

When Jesus spoke these words to Simon, it probably appeared to the others that the traitor had been revealed:

"Simon, Simon, behold, Satan has demanded permission to sift you like wheat; but I have prayed for you, that your faith may not fail; and you, when once you have turned again, strengthen your brothers." (vv. 31–32)

First, unbeknownst to the disciples, Satan had entered Judas. Now Jesus revealed the next step in Satan's evil plan—to try to destroy the Rock.

Notice that here, Jesus twice refers to Peter by his former name, Simon. He knew that the Rock would fail. Still, He offered His apostle hope by exhorting him: "once you have turned again, strengthen your brothers." Jesus knew that Simon would deny Him, but also that he would turn back to the Lord and be used to encourage his brethren. Peter was already forgiven for his future transgression.

You can imagine Simon Peter's chagrin at these words from Jesus. He immediately responded by declaring, "Lord, with You I am ready to go both to prison and to death!" (v. 33). Eugene Peterson's *The Message* renders the words, "Master, I'm ready for anything with you. I'd go to jail for you. I'd *die* for you!"[3] Another gospel says, "Even though all may fall away, yet I will not" (Mark 14:29).

Though embarrassed in front of his peers, Peter did not want to be proven a coward. In his impetuousness, he underestimated the gravity of the situation and overestimated his courage and loyalty to Christ. Peter set himself up for failure. And Jesus let him know this with the following words:

> "I say to you, Peter, the rooster will not crow today until you have denied three times that you know Me." (Luke 22:34)

Simon Peter Fails

Peter tried to prove his loyalty in the garden with a sword (see Mark 14:47). But as the soldiers arrested Jesus and the terrifying events of that night began to unfold, Simon's courage waned:

> Having arrested Him, they led Him away and brought Him to the house of the high priest; but Peter was following at a distance. (Luke 22:54)

---

3. Eugene Peterson, *The Message* (Colorado Springs, Colo.: NavPress, 1996), p. 177.

He wasn't grabbing the sword any longer. He wasn't clinging loyally to Christ as they dragged Him off to the royal court or demanding: "If you take Him, you take me. One for all and all for one!" No, instead Peter lurked in the shadows, his courage rebuffed by the glint of armor in the moonlight.

Like three jabs to the gut, the denials came quickly. Peter sought anonymity in a crowd that had congregated around a fire. But he separated himself even further from the accused Christ when a servant girl recognized him as one of Jesus' followers:

> And a servant-girl, seeing him as he sat in the fire-light and looking intently at him, said, "This man was with Him too." But he denied it, saying, "Woman, I do not know Him." (vv. 56–57)

As the night wore on, others recognized Peter as someone who had been with Christ:

> A little later, another saw him and said, "You are one of them too!" But Peter said, "Man, I am not!" (v. 58)

Peter's denials were motivated by his concern for his own personal safety. But, try as he might to avoid being associated with Jesus, people continued to press their case. It didn't take long for someone else in the crowd to pick out Peter's distinct Galilean accent:

> After about an hour had passed, another man began to insist, saying, "Certainly this man also was with Him, for he is a Galilean too." But Peter said, "Man, I do not know what you are talking about." (vv. 59–60)

One gospel writer says Peter swore and cursed to let everyone know he couldn't care less about this man, Jesus (Mark 14:71). But as the vehement protests left his lips, they were quickly drowned out by a sound in the distance:

> Immediately, while he was still speaking, a rooster crowed. (v. 60)

What happened next must have sent an arrow straight through Peter's heart:

> The Lord turned and looked at Peter. And Peter remembered the word of the Lord, how He had told

him, "Before a rooster crows today, you will deny Me three times." (v. 61)

With that single penetrating look from Jesus, Peter knew that he had failed. He had turned his back on his Master and Lord, the very same One whom he had pronounced earlier as "the Christ, the Son of the living God" (Matt. 16:16).

Peter's shattered promises and denials of His Lord overwhelmed him, "and he went out and wept bitterly" (v. 62). Eugene Peterson's paraphrase states, "He went out and cried and cried and cried" (THE MESSAGE).[4] The brash vows he had made hours earlier flooded his memory. His overconfident words only served to make his repeated denials of Christ more painful.

Peter, the burly fisherman, sat weeping in a back alley. His calloused hands cradled his face as tears of despair streamed down his face and formed a muddy pool in the dust. We don't know if he ever told his wife and the other disciples of his betrayal, or if he alone bore this yoke of despair. But one thing is clear—Peter was desperately sorry for his failure. His penitent heart and humble spirit allowed him to be reconciled to Jesus and to find favor with Him once more.

Hope for Our Dark Hours

Peter left the fire a failure. However, when Jesus rose from the grave, He singled out Peter once again. When Mary Magdalene and Mary the mother of James came to the tomb, an angel met them, saying, "Go, tell his disciples *and Peter*" (Mark 16:7, emphasis added). He did not say, "Go tell his disciples and *Simon*," but "tell Peter"—Peter, the Rock.

The Lord gave Peter a second chance, and this man grew to become one of the great apostles, a giant in the faith. Christ, in His mercy, forgave Peter's sin and wiped away all his tears. The Hebrews called this kind of love *hesed*, a term which meant "lovingkindness, loyalty, and steadfast love."

Though at times we falter like Peter did, God offers us His guiding hand. Though we fail, He remains loyal. Though we are fickle followers, He is steadfast. Regardless of our failures, regardless of how long we have been running from God, He awaits our return with open arms.

4. Peterson, *The Message*, p. 179.

You can choose to live like Peter after the cock crowed or like Peter after Pentecost. Rather than brood over his failures, he penitently accepted the Lord's tender mercy. And toward the end of his life, Peter, destined to become a martyr for the early church, exhorted his readers, "According to His great mercy the Lord has caused us to be born again to a living hope through the resurrection of Jesus Christ from the dead, and to obtain an inheritance which is imperishable and undefiled and will not fade away, reserved in heaven for you" (1 Peter 1:3–4). As the sun dawned anew and the rooster crowed each morning, Peter understood "great mercy" like few others.

Have you experienced failure like Peter? Perhaps you have yelled at your kids or spoken harshly to your spouse. Maybe you haven't kept your word. Maybe you have compromised your integrity at work to make a buck. You may have downplayed your relationship with Christ before skeptical friends. Let's face it—we've all failed royally! But fortunately for Peter and for us, our failures do not have to define us or linger as a debilitating presence in our lives.

We know that Jesus, our Savior, died on the cross and rose from the dead to give us new life and new hope in Him. He prays for us and mediates for us before the Father. And He offers us forgiveness when we come to Him with penitent hearts. Despite our failures, He provides us with hope and a new future.

 Living Insights

One of the most demoralizing experiences for children can be the process of picking teams. "Sarah, you're on my team!" "Josh, over here." "We want Jake!" Kids right and left are called, while others humbly hold up the wall and stare at their shoes. Finally, one captain of the kickball team says reluctantly, "Okay, Johnny, I guess you're on our team." Nothing like the obligatory slot on the bench to bolster confidence.

That's how John Mark might have felt when Barnabas and Paul were in a heated debate over whether or not he had a place on the second missionary team. Likely, he looked down and sheepishly kicked his feet in the dirt when Paul brought up the whole "desertion" issue that had occurred back in Pamphylia on the first missionary journey (Acts 15:38). Did one mistake mean John Mark was no longer valuable to the kingdom?

Barnabas chose to mend John Mark's wings rather than let him

9

flounder, while Paul felt he was too much of a liability. Thus two close friends parted company. But toward the end of Paul's life, when he penned his last letter in a Roman prison, he urged Timothy, "Pick up Mark and bring him with you, for he is useful to me for service" (2 Tim. 4:11). Thankfully, John Mark was no longer defined by his failure. In fact, he will be remembered forever for writing the second gospel!

Our mistakes do not disqualify us from God's love or His plan. Failures do not ruin our ability to serve the Lord. Problems do not undermine our eternal significance. Remember: All have sinned and fall short of the glory of God! Satan may shoot nagging darts into your heart, telling you that you're useless and that your failures are too great. But God heals your wounds. He turns your failures into footsteps toward His grace and power.

Take a few moments and write down your thoughts from these passages:

1 John 1:9 _____

_____

_____

_____

Psalm 32:5–7 _____

_____

_____

_____

Isaiah 44:22–23 _____

_____

_____

_____

2 Corinthians 12:9–10 _____

_____

_____

_____

Your personal struggles and failures will not thwart God's ultimate purpose for you! Isn't that great news? Take some time now to pray that, through God's grace, you might find new strength in the areas of your weakness, new confidence where there is doubt, and new hope where there is dismay. You can have the victory through Christ Jesus!

Small Group Insights

People hate to admit failure. When Adam and Eve failed, their first response was to try to shift the blame and hide their sin from God.

In the same way, many of us trudge through life lugging a suitcase full of failures. Often, we refuse to share our weaknesses with anyone. We try to hide them from God, from our loved ones, from those at church—and even from ourselves. So we end up carrying burdens that the Lord never intended for us to carry.

Jesus invited us to share our burdens with Him when He said, "Come to Me, all who are weary and heavy-laden, and I will give you rest. Take My yoke upon you and learn from Me, for I am gentle and humble in heart, and you will find rest for your souls. For My yoke is easy and My burden is light" (Matt. 11:28–30).

In your groups, take time to share a personal failure or burden that you have been carrying. It may be something in your past or an issue with which you are still struggling. Then pair off to pray for one another. Release your burdens to the Lord and trust Him to carry them for you!

Chapter 2

NEW HOPE
THROUGH FIERY TRIALS

1 Peter 1:3–9; Selected Scriptures

Suffering is a universal language. Despite our diversity, we all know what it means to hurt. But the causes for our pain vary. Sometimes we ache because a trusted spouse, colleague, friend, or family member has hurt us. In other instances, an unexpected tragedy like a natural disaster, a sudden layoff, or an illness may turn our worlds upside-down. And sometimes, we dig our own pit of despair by making sinful choices.

Many of our forerunners in the faith suffered as a result of their sin. Moses never entered the Promised Land because he could not control his anger. Samson lost his eyes and his strength because he could not control his libido. Even King David failed royally by committing adultery with Bathsheba and having her husband murdered. Simon Peter experienced deep despair after he denied Christ.

These people followed God but were also profoundly human, committing sins that scarred their lives forever. Deep guilt and pain followed as a result. F. B. Meyer stated, "This is the bitterest of all, to know that suffering need not have been; that it has resulted from indiscretion and inconsistency, that the vulture which feeds on the vitals is the nestling of one's own rearing. Ah me, this is pain."[1]

Suffering slices through even the toughest emotional armor. Unseen trials lurk inside the homes of your neighbors; pain percolates inside each person you see on your morning commute. Perhaps a personal tragedy threatens to break through the façade you have been trying to present to friends and coworkers. When God seems to be turning up the heat in your life, where can you turn? Let's examine a group of believers who were feeling the heat and see how they found new hope.

---

1. F. B. Meyer, *Christ in Isaiah,* as quoted by Charles R. Swindoll in *The Tale of the Tardy Oxcart and 1,501 Other Stories* (Nashville, Tenn.: Word Publishing, Inc., 1998), p. 549.

A Grim Reality

Peter's letter that has come to be known as the book of 1 Peter addressed an amalgamation of Gentile and Jewish believers scattered throughout Asia Minor—a people of distinct cultures, varied geographical settings, and contrasting backgrounds. Peter wrote:

> Peter, an apostle of Jesus Christ,
> To those who reside as aliens, scattered throughout
> Pontus, Galatia, Cappadocia, Asia, and Bithynia.
> (1 Peter 1:1)

Because Peter penned this letter in Greek, the common language of the day, his broad audience could immediately understand it. The letter addressed the issue of suffering, and Peter's persecuted audience identified deeply with the message:

> Beloved, do not be surprised at the fiery ordeal among you, which comes upon you for your testing, as though some strange thing were happening to you; but to the degree that you share the sufferings of Christ, keep on rejoicing, so that also at the revelation of His glory you may rejoice with exultation (4:12 – 13).

For Christians in that day, life was grim indeed. The violent and capricious emperor Nero was in power. Nero suffered from mental disorders and had virtually everyone close to him murdered, including his own mother.[2] He felt threatened by those who believed in Jesus and made life as miserable as possible for them.

In A.D. 64, a great fire razed Rome. The Christians became a convenient scapegoat, though many scholars believe Nero himself ignited the fire out of boredom or to divert the attention of his critics. Many Christians perished under Nero's merciless persecution. Two of Christianity's most honored leaders, Peter and Paul, were martyred during his reign.[3]

---

2. *The New Bible Dictionary*, (Wheaton, Ill.: Tyndale House Publishers, Inc., 1962), see "Nero"; accessed through the Logos Library System.

3. Ronald F. Youngblood, F. F. Bruce, and R. K. Harrison, eds., *Nelson's New Illustrated Bible Dictionary*, (Nashville, Tenn.: Thomas Nelson Publishers, 1995, 1986); accessed through the Logos Library System.

Clearly, the Christians within the Roman Empire who Peter was addressing were experiencing great pressure. Regarded as counter-cultural, they were maliciously victimized, ostracized by Roman society, and ruthlessly hunted as traitors.

Peter encouraged these persecuted believers by reminding them of the elements of their faith:

> To those who are chosen . . . according to the foreknowledge of God the Father, by the sanctifying work of the Spirit, to obey Jesus Christ and be sprinkled with His blood: May grace and peace be yours in the fullest measure. (1 Peter 1:1–2)

Peter later referred to his readers as being "tested by fire" (1:7) and enduring a "fiery ordeal" (4:12). He recognized that maturity in the lives of believers would not come without pain. This is still true today. The furnace of trials refines our hearts and sanctifies our spirits. Christians should not be surprised at suffering; we should expect it! But we can have a new and lasting hope, no matter what circumstances we may face.

Six Reasons We Can Make It

In the book of James, which precedes Peter's first epistle, James tells us to "consider it all joy, my brethren, when you encounter various trials" (1:2). Rejoice, even in suffering? It seems that these persecuted believers had little cause for rejoicing. But Peter provided them with six reasons to have joy and hope when the stakes were high.

We Have a Living Hope

> Blessed be the God and Father of our Lord Jesus Christ, who according to His great mercy has caused us to be born again to a living hope through the resurrection of Jesus Christ from the dead. (1 Peter 1:3)

Underline the word *living*. We are born again to a hope that's active and alive. Our hope rests upon the person of Christ. This does not mean that we simply wish for a better future in a chaotic and unpredictable world. Biblical hope is not based upon a future event or wishful thinking. We possess a tangible hope that is solidly founded on the work of Christ. God carried His Son through the excruciating events of the crucifixion and snatched Him from the

14

grip of death itself, so He certainly has the power to bring us through whatever we face. And that's our basis for true hope!

We Have a Permanent Inheritance

> . . . to obtain an inheritance which is imperishable and undefiled and will not fade away, reserved in heaven for you . . . (v. 4)

Our ultimate home is heaven. And our place there was reserved for us by our heavenly Father and purchased by His Son, Jesus Christ. Our earthly homes and the possessions we work so hard to gain will all fade away. But nothing can destroy our home in heaven. Though life on earth may be difficult and uncertain, our eternal home is sure.

We Have Divine Protection

> . . . who are protected by the power of God through faith for a salvation ready to be revealed in the last time. (v. 5)

Under heaven's lock and key, we are protected by the most efficient security system available—the power of God. Nothing catches Him by surprise. There is no way that we will be lost in the process of suffering, no matter how acute our pain may be. No disorder, no disease, not even death itself can steal away God's ultimate protection over our lives.

We Have a Developing Faith

> In this you greatly rejoice, even though now for a little while, if necessary, you have been distressed by various trials, so that the proof of your faith, being more precious than gold which is perishable, even though tested by fire, may be found to result in praise and glory and honor at the revelation of Jesus Christ. (vv. 6 – 7)

Several times in his letter Peter refers to "rejoicing." The words *even though* indicate that the joy is unconditional and does not depend on the circumstances surrounding us. We can rejoice even in our sufferings because we know that they make us more mature and faithful followers of Christ.

These verses also teach us three significant principles about suffering. First, trials are necessary because they prove the genuineness of our faith and teach us humility. Second, they stir compassion within us so that we sympathize with others who are hurting. And third, trials come in various forms.[4]

This variety of trials is like different temperature settings on God's furnace. The settings are adjusted to burn off our impurities, temper us, or soften us, according to what meets our highest need. It is in God's refining fires that the authenticity of our faith is revealed. The purpose of these fiery ordeals is that we come forth as purified gold, a shining likeness of the Lord Jesus Himself. Our reflection of Him is what ultimately gives glory and praise and honor to Christ.

We Have an Unseen Savior

> Though you have not seen Him, you love Him, and though you do not see Him now, but believe in Him, you greatly rejoice with joy inexpressible and full of glory. (v. 8)

Peter gives us doctrine we can sink our teeth into, not a little theological hors d'oeuvre. He reminds us that our Savior loves us and that He is standing with us throughout whatever trials we may face.

Some, like the disciple Thomas, needed to see and touch Jesus in order to believe. The Savior's words to the doubting disciple are instructive: "Blessed are they who did not see, and yet believed" (John 20:29). Even though we can't see Jesus beside us in our trials, He is there (Ps. 23:4; Matt. 28:20; Heb. 13:5).

We Have a Guaranteed Deliverance

> . . . obtaining as the outcome of your faith the salvation of your souls. (1 Peter 1:9)

The final result of our faith is the deliverance of our souls, which includes not only a deliverance from our present struggles with sin and circumstances, but also a glorification of our physical bodies.

Regarding Salvation: Why Prophets Were Curious

With the mention of this salvation or deliverance, Peter takes us on a literary interlude in which he addresses some questions that

---

4. See Psalm 66:10; Proverbs 17:3; Isaiah 43:2 – 3; and especially Isaiah 48:8 – 11 in which God describes a testing in the "furnace of affliction" (Isa. 48:10).

may have been under discussion in Christian circles in that day. Believers must have been asking him questions such as: What about earlier times, in the days of the prophets? Did they grasp the full significance of this salvation? If not, how much did they comprehend? These questions are answered in verses 10–12:

> As to this salvation, the prophets who prophesied of the grace that would come to you made careful searches and inquiries, seeking to know what person or time the Spirit of Christ within them was indicating as He predicted the sufferings of Christ and the glories to follow. It was revealed to them that they were not serving themselves, but you, in these things which now have been announced to you through those who preached the gospel to you by the Holy Spirit sent from heaven—things into which angels long to look.

We're told here that the prophets wrote of the sufferings of Christ and of the glory that would ultimately be His. But verse 10 concludes that these prophets "made careful searches and inquiries." Why? Because they didn't have access to two critical privileges that we have today.

First: *They didn't have a clear picture of God's full plan.* Looking ahead, they saw two mountain peaks—Mount Calvary and Mount Olivet. On one, Christ would die in disgrace; on the other, He would return in glory. What they couldn't see from their vantage point was that between these two mountains stretched a valley representing the present church age, an era when God would extend His grace to the Gentiles.

Second: *They didn't have the Holy Spirit living within them as we do today.* The Holy Spirit of God spoke *to* and *through* the prophets. He inspired them and ignited their message like a fire from heaven. But the benefits of the permanent indwelling of the Spirit were a total mystery to the prophets. Like a blind lamplighter faithfully making his rounds on the streets of seventeenth-century London, a prophet lit lamps for the benefit of others, not himself. Only later, after Christ ascended to heaven, was the Spirit sent to dwell in the lives of believers.

A Personal Word

Right now, you may be suffering under the weight of your trials. Or you may be searching for answers.

To those who are suffering: Only Christ's perspective can replace your resentment with rejoicing. Jesus is the central piece of suffering's puzzle. If you fit Him into place, the rest of the puzzle—no matter how dark and enigmatic—begins to make sense. That's when the rejoicing first begins to replace resentment.

To those who are seeking: Only Christ's salvation can change you from a spectator to a participant. Don't just sit in the audience, watching. Step out of your seat and onto the stage! You, too, can play a part in the unfolding drama of redemption. The scenes will be demanding: some triumphant, some tragic. But once you become a follower of Christ, you will better understand the roles that both joy and suffering play in your life. And only then will you find new hope through fiery trials.

 Living Insights

A single mom with four kids and no job needs more than a verse to make it through her long days. A weeping girl who just lost her best friend needs more than a hug and a book on God's promises. Parents burying their stillborn child may wonder where God is and if He will see them through. A man who was fired holds up a sign "Will work for food. Can you help?"

Our struggles are real; they are hard, and they can't be eliminated with trite platitudes. We need an anchor, a hope beyond the fiery ordeals of life. We desperately need proper perspective when suffering saps our strength. What Scripture provides for us is not a panacea for pain, but a solid foundation for living. Nowhere else in this world will you find true comfort or peace in the midst of personal pain. Simply trust God to be who He is, and follow His Word.

Read the verses listed below.

Isaiah 43:2   John 16:33   James 1:2

What is the common thread in these verses? _____

_____

_____

The writers of Scripture maintained that our suffering identifies us with Christ. It shapes our spirit and cultivates our character. When we ask God to remove our struggles, we may be requesting Him to remove the very things He is using to craft us into His image.

Paul asked three times for God to remove a thorn from his life. The thorn remained, but Paul realized it was used to prick his pride and portray God's power (2 Cor. 12:7). Paul stated, "And He said to me, 'My grace is sufficient for you, for power is perfected in weakness'" (12:9). God does not promise us a reprieve from pain in this world. But He does promise He will be present in the fiery furnace.

Jesus did not turn to his disciples in the garden of Gethsemane and say, "Don't worry; be happy." Sweat poured from His body like drops of blood. He understood the weight, the gravity of pain.

In the same way, God does not ask us to abandon our pain and replace it with a superficial veneer of joy. The joy comes in the quiet, resolute moments when we realize He truly is in control. Peace passes understanding not at the conclusion of a trial, but in the very midst of it when we rest in His sufficiency. We rejoice because we stand resolute in the truth that "neither death, nor life, nor angels, nor principalities, nor things present, nor things to come, nor powers, nor height, nor depth, nor any other created thing, will be able to separate us from the love of God which is in Christ Jesus our Lord" (Rom. 8:38–39).

Cry out to God. Write a lament prayer in which you bare your soul to Him and reveal to Him your very real emotions. As you finish, reaffirm the truth of Scripture: He will never leave you nor forsake you (see Heb. 13:15).

ᨊ Small Group Insights

Like the word *love*, the word *fellowship* may have many definitions in our culture. We hear it when a church meeting promises "food, fun, and *fellowship*." We see it as we enter the church's multi-purpose room, the *Fellowship* Hall. But the Greek word for fellowship, *koinonia*, connotes "association, communion [or] close relationship."[5] Biblical *koinonia* indicates a group of people intentionally pursuing a depth of relationship marked by personal sacrifice and intimacy.

Take some time to read these verses aloud:

- Acts 2:42 – 47
- Ephesians 4:1 – 6
- Philippians 2:1 – 4
- James 5:13 – 16, 19 – 20
- 1 John 1:3 – 4

Answer the following questions as a group.

1. How are our relationships within the church different from other relationships in the world?

2. How does God provide an outlet for those who are bearing burdens?

Individually, write down your answers to the following questions.

1. When a crisis hits, with whom do you share your feelings and your struggles?

_____

_____

_____

_____

---

5. See William F. Arndt and F. Wilbur Gingrich, eds., *A Greek-English Lexicon of the New Testament and other Early Christian Literature*, 2d ed., revised and augmented (Chicago, Ill.: University of Chicago Press, 1957, 1979), p. 438.

2. How do some people in the church put up a façade? Why do you think they do this?

_____

_____

_____

3. On a scale of 1 – 5, with 5 being the best, how easy do you find it to share with the people in your church? Circle one.

1   2   3   4   5

4. On a scale of 1 – 5, how easy do you find it to share with others in your small group? Circle one.

1   2   3   4   5

5. Would you be willing to share a personal burden with this group? If so, write it down so the group may lift you up in prayer.

_____

_____

_____

6. How could the church, and specifically this group, create an atmosphere conducive to vulnerability?

_____

_____

_____

Now, look back over the previous verses and pick a theme verse for the group. Let it prompt you to foster future *koinonia*.

Chapter 3

NEW HOPE
WHEN LIFE AIN'T FAIR
1 Peter 2:11 – 25; Selected Scriptures

Enduring unfair treatment is tough. Perhaps you got passed over for that promotion you wanted so badly or lost your job when the company downsized. Maybe your spouse has hurt you or you have lost a child due to illness or an accident. When hard times come and we don't have the answers, we cry out to God about the unfairness of it all. But sometimes He seems silent when we want Him so desperately to speak to us in our need.

We *want* life to be fair. We want what is right to be valued and honored. We long for the happy ending where evil is exposed and defeated. We admire people who endure pain and difficult circumstances that they don't deserve—we just don't want to be one of them!

Remember David? He trusted God and killed a giant. But, as his popularity rose and the Israelite people began to sing songs in his honor, King Saul became jealous. The refrain "Saul has slain his thousands, and David his ten thousands" echoed in the enraged king's ears as he began to treat David more and more unfairly and even tried to kill him on multiple occasions.

David had several opportunities to avenge this unfair treatment by killing Saul, but he honorably refused to destroy the Lord's anointed. We admire David for his self-control, just as we marvel at patient Job's ability to withstand severe illness, despair, and the loss of his entire family. But we're thankful that we aren't in David's or Job's shoes. We know that "life just ain't fair," but what can we do about it? Let's see what Peter had to say on the subject of enduring unfair treatment.

We're Not in Kansas Anymore

> Beloved, I urge you as aliens and strangers to abstain from fleshly lusts which wage war against the soul. (1 Peter 2:11)

This chapter has been adapted from "Pressing On Even Though Ripped Off," in the Bible study guide *Hope in Hurtful Times*, written by Ken Gire, from the Bible-teaching ministry of Charles R. Swindoll (Anaheim, Calif.: Insight for Living, 1990), pp. 46–53.

Peter began this section by addressing his audience as "beloved," or "dear friends" in some translations. His audience included believers who were Jewish, Gentile, slave, free, and even full-fledged Roman citizens. But regardless of their official status, once they trusted Christ, they became "aliens and strangers" in this temporal world. In the Roman context, Christians were viewed at best with caution and at worst as bitter enemies. Peter spoke plainly: once you pledge allegiance to Christ, you enter a hostile world.

In light of this troubling fact, Peter exhorted believers "to abstain from fleshly lusts." He wanted them to keep themselves pure from sexual sin and to resist the temptation to react to a hostile world with fleshly responses. Peter's teaching halted the people's hunger for retribution when their rights had been trampled and injustice was running rampant. Why? Because enduring unfairness did not just test their mettle. It served a higher purpose — evangelism.

> Keep your behavior excellent among the Gentiles, so that in the thing in which they slander you as evildoers, they may because of your good deeds, as they observe them, glorify God in the day of visitation. (v. 12)

Remember the plight of Peter's audience? These Christians faced "various trials" (1 Peter 1:6) and a "fiery ordeal" (4:12). Some scholars believe "the persecution in view is the kind carried out not with fire and sword but with words — words of ridicule, slander and sometimes formal accusations of crimes against society."[1]

Peter was probably writing this letter around A.D. 64, during the era of persecution under Nero. At that time, slanderous accusations against Christians often translated into coliseum appearances. Believers were forced to meet secretly in catacombs—maze-like underground burial places. Such trials must have caused some new believers to question the notion of divine justice.

Peter, knowing his audience wondered how such a loving God could permit such blatant unfairness, wrote to offer new hope. Often the Lord does not provide a *way out* of trials, but a *way through*.

---

1. *Dictionary of the Later New Testament*, ed. Ralph P. Martin and Peter H. Davids (Downers Grove, Ill.: InterVarsity Press, 1997), p. 919.

An Alternative Response to Unfair Treatment

Facing an antagonistic world can be daunting. Most people respond to injustice in one of three ways. Some respond aggressively by blaming authorities, the source of injustice, or even God for allowing such struggles. Others respond passively by feeling sorry for themselves and creating cocoons of self-pity. And still others postpone dealing with the problem by burying their emotions and trying to ignore the injustice.

However, Peter provided a jarring alternative — one that defies our natural tendencies and common sense. It goes against the grain of our natural desires, but it's also the only solution that works. Peter presented new hope with one word: *submission.*

A Lesson on Submission

Peter challenged his audience to respond to unfair treatment by practicing *hupotasso*—the Greek term for submission. *Hupotasso* is composed of two Greek words, *tasso*, meaning "to appoint, order, or arrange," and *hupo*, meaning "to place under or to subordinate." It's a military term meaning "to arrange [troop divisions] in a military fashion under the command of a leader." In non-military use, it involves "a voluntary attitude of giving in, cooperating, assuming responsibility, and carrying a burden."[2] *Hupotasso* suggests a willing effort to bring one's own personal preferences and desires under the submission of an accepted authority.

Peter first reminded believers to practice *hupotasso* in respect to the government (1 Peter 2:13 – 17). Next, he challenged slaves to submit to their masters (2:18 – 20), illustrating the way Christ submitted even to those who treated Him cruelly (2:21 – 25). Peter began chapter 3 with an exhortation for wives to submit to their husbands (3:1 – 6). He then called upon men to treat their wives with understanding and honor so that their prayers would not be hindered (3:7). Finally, Peter addressed all believers by exhorting them to submit to one another in love (3:8 – 9).

Let's examine each of these passages more closely to discover Peter's strategy for teaching submission. *Hupotasso* may not be an easy task, but it's the only answer to the unfairness of life.

---

2. *Enhanced Strong's Lexicon* (Ontario, Canada: Woodside Bible Fellowship, 1995, 1996), see "hupotasso"; accessed through the Logos Library System.

Submit to the Government

The Command

Submit yourselves for the Lord's sake to every human institution, whether to a king as the one in authority, or to governors as sent by him for the punishment of evildoers and the praise of those who do right. (1 Peter 2:13 – 14)

When facing an antagonistic government set upon the destruction of Christians, should believers take up their swords and revolt? Peter said no. Nowhere in Scripture is anarchy promoted. This does not mean we buckle under by compromising our convictions or renouncing our faith. It means that we offer our respect to those in authority. It means we are not only to pray for our leaders (1 Tim. 2:1 – 2), but we are also to live honorably under their dominion (Rom. 13:1 – 3).

The Reason

For such is the will of God that by doing right you may silence the ignorance of foolish men. (1 Peter 2:15)

The Greek word for *silence* means "to close the mouth with a muzzle." By submitting honorably to the ruling governments, we muzzle our critics. It seems that throughout the Roman Empire many rumors were being spread about Christians — about their secret meetings, their unusual customs, their subversive ideologies, their loyalty to another kingdom, and their plans to lead an insurrection.

To muzzle these rumors, Peter encouraged submission to those in authority. Christians, bought with a price, have the freedom to act as no other people in the world — *righteously*. Peter exhorted believers to act on that freedom by honoring and paying homage to the king (vv. 16 – 17).

Submit to Masters

The Command

Servants, be submissive to your masters with all respect, not only to those who are good and gentle, but also to those who are unreasonable. (v. 18)

25

Submission to the government is one thing. But in verse 18, Peter got personal. In the Roman world, treatment of slaves varied from house to house. Peter made a distinction between good and unreasonable masters, but he makes no distinction as to how slaves were to treat either type. He exhorted slaves to "be submissive . . . with all respect."

Take a moment to look in a window at Roman slavery:

> Many slaves were loved and trusted members of the family; but one great inescapable fact dominated the whole situation. In Roman law a slave was not a person but a thing; and he had absolutely no legal rights whatsoever. . . . The only difference between a slave and a beast or a farmyard cart is that a slave happened to be able to speak. Peter Chrysologus sums the matter up: "Whatever a master does to a slave, undeservedly, in anger, willingly, unwillingly, in forgetfulness, after careful thought, knowingly, unknowingly, is judgment, justice, and law."[3]

Why wasn't Peter concerned with abolition, freedom for slaves, and social justice? The Scriptures weren't immediately concerned with changing the social order; they were concerned with the greater priority, which was changing the human heart (see 1 Cor. 7:20–24).

The Reason

> For this finds favor, if for the sake of conscience toward God a person bears up under sorrows when suffering unjustly. For what credit is there if, when you sin and are harshly treated, you endure it with patience? But if when you do what is right and suffer for it you patiently endure it, this finds favor with God. (1 Peter 2:19–20)

Peter used a unique phrase in this verse. "For this finds favor" literally means "for this is *grace.*" Believers who faithfully endure injustice receive the *grace of God.*

We'd all have been delighted to carry the bags of Mother Teresa or to wait on a man like Billy Graham. However, Peter emphasized

---

3. William Barclay, *The Letters of James and Peter,* rev. ed., The Daily Study Bible Series (Philadelphia, Pa.: Westminster Press, 1976), p. 11.

that believers receive favor when they serve the reprobate, the capricious, and the unjust—with the same fervor as they would the righteous.

Peter masterfully illustrated the startling command Jesus gave early in his earthly ministry: "Love your enemies" (Luke 6:35). Peter put flesh on this goal by demonstrating how it can be applied to the institutions of government and slavery. One commentator notes, "The ethical thrust of the epistle is to equate the radical command to love one's enemies with the doing of good in a variety of social situations in Roman society."[4]

The Ultimate Example

At the pinnacle of submission stands the example of Christ:

> For you have been called for this purpose, since Christ also suffered for you, leaving you an example for you to follow in His steps. (1 Peter 2:21)

If our eyes consistently peer through the lens of human perspective, we can lose sight of our example, Jesus. We may plot personal vengeance, slip into self-pity, or bury ourselves in an avalanche of bitterness. However, as Peter pointed out, to endure unjust suffering is part of our calling, our purpose, and our example to a fallen world. We must keep walking with our eyes focused on Christ.

Peter remembered the yoke of unjust suffering that was placed upon Jesus' shoulders. He saw firsthand the rejection by society and the retaliation of the Sanhedrin. He witnessed how a fickle empire brutalized an innocent man. One of his friends betrayed Jesus with a kiss. Peter himself denied Christ in His hour of greatest need. Yet Jesus harbored no revenge. His eyes reflected mercy rather than malice. His lips uttered, "Father, forgive them; for they do not know what they are doing" (Luke 23:34). After His resurrection, Jesus treated his betrayers to breakfast rather than bitterness (John 21).

What's Your Mountain?

If you find yourself climbing the steep mountain of unjust suffering, realize you are not the only sheep enduring the wilds of

4. J. Ramsey Michaels, 1 Peter, vol. 49 of Word Biblical Commentary, ed. David A. Hubbard, Glen W. Barker, and Ralph P. Martin (Dallas, Tex.: Word Books, 1998); accessed through the Logos Library System.

unfairness. Look up to the pinnacle and you will find your Shepherd:

> For you were continually straying like sheep, but now you have returned to the Shepherd and Guardian of your souls. (1 Peter 2:25)

The Guardian of our souls is our comfort, our example. As humans, we can't stomach the thought of enduring pain for another's malice. We cry, "It's not my fault. It's not right. It's not fair!" Not only does God see all, we are promised He protects those He loves. But protection does not necessarily mean the absence of injustice. David, Job, and Joseph all suffered while under the watchful eye of God. We will never be able to control our circumstances, only our reactions. And, we know that God will be with us no matter what we may face.

Finally, Peter addressed all believers by exhorting them to submit to one another in love:

> To sum up, all of you be harmonious, sympathetic, brotherly, kindhearted, and humble in spirit; not returning evil for evil or insult for insult, but giving a blessing instead; for you were called for the very purpose that you might inherit a blessing. (3:8 – 9)

If we call ourselves Jesus' disciples, we will bear some splinters of a cross of unjust suffering. Our bosses may ridicule our beliefs. Our houses may be broken into and the thieves never caught. Our spouses may acquire an inexplicable terminal illness. Our missionaries may be brutalized for sharing the Good News. Vindication may not come in this world, but it will come in the next. The psalmist exhorts us, "Let the mountains sing together for joy / Before the Lord, for He is coming to judge the earth; / He will judge the world with righteousness / And the peoples with equity" (Psalm 98:8).

 Living Insights

At times, Peter himself suffered from a narrow viewpoint. You may remember "Peter's Finest Hour" from chapter 1 of this study. Peter's perspective on the unfair treatment Christ prophesied about Himself incited Jesus' anger. Just after Peter shared his inspired word about Jesus, he changed from devotee to dissenter.

Read Matthew 16:21 – 23.

What prophecy did Jesus reveal to His disciples? _____

_____

_____

How did Peter respond? _____

_____

How did Christ respond to Peter? _____

_____

_____

How does Peter's response compare to your own reaction to God when injustice or unfairness strikes you? Or when you feel like God Himself is being unfair?

_____

_____

What steps can you take today to ensure that you will respond God's way next time?

_____

_____

_____

Small Group Insights

Joseph overcame the odds more than once. At the beginning of Genesis 39, we find him at the head of the household of Potiphar, a wealthy and powerful Egyptian. Successful and blessed by God, Joseph had triumphed over the injustice heaped upon him by his brothers. His only "curse" was being young, tall, dark, and handsome (39:6).

While his older brother Judah slept with an incognito daughter-in-law (Gen. 38), Joseph found himself standing trial for a crime he did not commit. In the absence of DNA testing or a great detective like Perry Mason, Joseph's torn garment in the hands of Potiphar's scheming wife was all it took to have him sentenced to the dungeon.

Divide your group into two smaller groups. Have one read Genesis 38 and the other Genesis 39. Afterward, ask these questions:

1. How are Joseph's and Judah's stories similar?

2. How are they different?

3. What can you glean about unfairness from these passages?

4. Take some time to discuss some experiences of injustice you may have encountered. How have they splintered your relationship with God or others?

5. What pattern do you find yourself slipping into when such struggles come?

6. Deep in the dungeon Joseph no doubt battled bitterness, maybe as often as he battled boredom. However, what was Joseph's response to the injustice demonstrated against him, both by his brothers and Potiphar's wife?

7. What have you learned about God's providence from these two passages?

Read aloud Genesis 45:1–15.

Highlight in your Bible those passages in which Joseph attributes his travails to the will of God. Maybe in your own life, the only reward you received for acting righteously was a heavy dose of injustice. Take heart, and join the company of those who have gone before you: Joseph, who was wrongfully accused; David, who was berated by a jealous king; Isaiah, who was literally sawn in half; Stephen, who was stoned by paranoid religious leaders; and of course our Savior, who was crucified for our sins. Remember, you can have hope in Christ, even when life isn't fair.

Chapter 4

NEW HOPE
FOR YOUR MARRIAGE

1 Peter 3:1–7

A wedding is one thing; a marriage is another. Weddings bring to mind soft music, rows of candles, beautiful attire, close friends and family members . . . all framed by vivid flowers in eternal bloom. But, as every married couple knows, the bliss of the wedding day cannot sustain a lifetime together. Usually, the honeymoon lasts about a week. Then the smooth ride often becomes a rough backpacking trip across treacherous mountains.

Author Joe Aldrich wrote, "It doesn't take long for the newlyweds to discover that 'everything in one person nobody's got.' They soon learn that a marriage license is just a learner's permit, and ask with agony, 'Is there life after marriage?'" Quoting another author, Aldrich continued, "the essential difficulties of life do not end, but rather begin with marriage."[1]

Sounds discouraging, doesn't it? Fortunately a letter written by Peter, who was not only a disciple of Jesus but a married man as well, offers new hope for the age-old struggle between two sinful people residing under the same roof.

In the last chapter, we examined Peter's teaching on submission. We learned that believers, as loyal citizens, should submit to governing authorities and that slaves should respond to their masters. We also paused to view the ultimate example of Christ's submission. Now we'll survey a true test of submission and love: relationships between husbands and wives.

Wise Counsel to Wives

> In the same way, you wives, be submissive to your own husbands . . . (1 Peter 3:1a)

We shouldn't assume simply because our Bibles indicate a new chapter, that Peter changed the subject here. The Greek term meaning

---

1. Joe Aldrich, *Secrets to Inner Beauty*, as quoted by Charles R. Swindoll in *The Tale of the Tardy Oxcart and 1,501 Other Stories* (Nashville, Tenn.: Word Publishing, 1998), p. 364.

"in the same manner" or "likewise" connects the first six verses of chapter 3 with the passage that began in 2:13 regarding submission to authority. Peter's new hope for marriages rested upon the ultimate example of Christ. Just as Jesus submitted to His Father's will, wives are called to willingly submit to their husbands in love.

Many wives' first reaction to that may be, "No problem, Peter. I'll willingly submit, as long as my husband is attentive, takes out the trash, plays with the children, doesn't turn on the TV the second he gets home, and of course, leads in a spiritually sensitive manner . . ." It's natural to have such a conditional response: "If my husband acts this way, then I will honor, serve, and love him faithfully." But Peter's directive is not meant only for women who are married to Prince Charming. God presents wives with a higher command, a spiritual perspective antithetical to the common response of the flesh.

> . . . so that even if any of them are disobedient to the word . . . (3:1b)

Peter implied that, at times, even the best of husbands may be callous, uncaring, inattentive, and yes, even disobedient to the Word of God. He addressed wives of couch potatoes, slackers, and the unsaved.

Look at the people who Peter has commanded in this letter to be submissive: citizens, slaves, and now wives. Historically, most citizens did not choose their kings. Slaves didn't choose their masters. And for the most part, wives did not choose their husbands. In the ancient Near East, arranged marriages were common, and most were based upon financial stability rather than romantic love. Therefore, wives in Peter's day faced a real challenge to submit.

As we learned in the last chapter, life can be unfair. Even today, many wives feel trapped in marriages that have lost their spark. Perhaps the tenderness and kindness in your own marriage have evaporated. Peter's letter has a word for you too. It offers you three practical ways to find new hope.

Analyze Your Actions

First, Peter prompted wives to analyze their own actions. Women who find themselves in the day-to-day grind of dealing with an unresponsive or even antagonistic husband may be tempted to respond by nagging, pouting, shaming, or manipulating. But there are two problems with such behavior. First, a nagging wife assumes a responsibility that is not hers: she's trying to change her husband. Secondly, she is spending her energy on the wrong person by focusing on her own needs rather than the needs of her husband.

An obedient wife chooses to love her husband unconditionally and refuses to play the shame and blame game. Consider the example of Billy and Ruth Graham. Though many women may think Billy Graham must be the perfect husband, he's still a sinful man. Yet, his wife says, "It's my job to love Billy. It's God's job to make him good."

Peter reflects the same sentiment as he suggests a radical approach for wives to follow:

> . . . [husbands] may be won without a word by the behavior of their wives, as they observe your chaste and respectful behavior. (1 Peter 3:1–2)

A wife's loving actions resonate more deeply than a sharp rebuke. The Greek word translated *observe* means "to give serious consideration to, suggesting the possibility of something unusual."[2] A wife's gracious service can disarm a callous husband and prompt him to ponder the mystery of her godly and quiet response.

Peter reveals the secret to changing a man's heart: let go and let God. The quiet submission of a godly wife will influence her husband more than bitter badgering. Divorce won't work; trying to change him won't work; and nagging tends to have the same effect as a leaky faucet (see Prov. 19:13; 27:15). But once a wife's kind actions wash away her objections, a husband will pause to listen.

Watch Your Attitude

Secondly, Peter exhorts wives to examine their attitudes.

> Your adornment must not be merely external — braiding the hair, and wearing gold jewelry, or putting on dresses . . . (1 Peter 3:3)

Now, before jumping to legalistic conclusions, realize this passage does not forbid women to visit the hair salon, put on jewelry, or wear dresses. Rather, it draws a sharp contrast between inner beauty and outer adornment:

> . . . but let it be the hidden person of the heart,

---

2. Johannes P. Louw and Eugene A. Nida, eds., *Greek-English Lexicon of the New Testament* (New York, N.Y.: United Bible Societies, 1988, 1989); accessed through Logos Library System.

with the imperishable quality of a gentle and quiet
spirit, which is precious in the sight of God. (3:4)

Peter contrasted external trappings with the internal marks of
a godly wife. He said that a woman should be recognized for her
"hidden person of the heart," meaning her strength of character.
While the world values a woman's beauty, youth, and physical
attributes, God sees the value of her heart and soul.

A "gentle and quiet spirit" highlights a woman's inner beauty.
The word *gentle* used here is also found in Matthew 5:5, where it
refers to those who will inherit the earth. And in Matthew 11:29,
this term is used to describe the meekness and gentleness of Christ.
Peter urged women to strive for eternal character, which is precious
in the sight of God. Peter echoed Proverbs 31:25, "Strength and
dignity are her clothing, and she smiles at the future."

Evaluate Your Attention

Finally, Peter advised wives to evaluate who receives their attention. As an illustration, he harked back to the heroines of old:

> For in this way in former times the holy women also,
> who hoped in God, used to adorn themselves, being
> submissive to their own husbands. (1 Peter 3:5)

No doubt Peter reviewed in his mind the stories of holy women
through the centuries: wives like Ruth, Hannah, and Esther. Such
women put their "hope," or security, in God rather than in a husband. These women adorned themselves with the robe of
submission—not slavishly, but willingly and respectfully. Peter then
turned to a specific example:

> . . . just as Sarah obeyed Abraham, calling him lord,
> and you have become her children if you do what
> is right without being frightened by any fear. (3:6)

Sarah called her husband "lord," even though Abraham was far
from perfect. In fact, Abraham was so cowardly that he was willing
to sacrifice his wife to another man, not just once, but twice! (see
Gen. 12:10–20; 20:1–18) Yet Sarah obeyed and respected Abraham. She adapted to Abraham's world, needs, and concerns. God
did not command Abraham to go alone to an unknown land; He
told Sarah to leave everything she held dear (family, friends, home)
and follow her husband. And Sarah simply followed without being

34

frightened. She attended to her husband's needs and trusted his God.

In this upside-down world in which men want to be more like women and women more like men, God says to both groups, "I made you different, but not indifferent. Plumb the depths of each other and appreciate the distinctions." It's amazing what can happen to a marriage when husbands and wives follow God's lead. Wives find the chinks in the emotional armor of their husbands when they intentionally honor and pay attention to them.

It may seem like Peter spent an undue amount of time writing to wives. After all, he penned six verses for wives, compared to just one for husbands. God knew that husbands needed simple, clear, and concise directions. And He knew that if men could master this next verse, women would be better able embrace the biblical model of submission.

Strong Guidelines for Husbands

When we read the Bible, we often tend to overlook transition words and rush ahead to find the "meat" of the verse. However, if you skip over the first words in this verse, you've bypassed the whole meal:

> You husbands in the same way . . . (3:7a)

"In the same way" could be translated "similarly" or "likewise." This phrase ties together Peter's entire message on submission. Just as citizens should dutifully serve the government; just as slaves should obey masters; just as Christ submitted to His Father; just as wives should submit to husbands, husbands are commanded to love their wives.

The Bible clarifies that husbands are heads of the family in the same way that Christ is head of the church (Eph. 5:23). *Head* does not translate in the Greek as "dictator," "tyrant," or "brute." While a wife's role in the family is to submit to her husband, a husband's role is to love his wife tenderly and care for her needs. Just as Christ sacrificed for the church, the husband should sacrifice for his wife. Peter outlined three very specific ways.

Live with Your Wife Intimately

> . . . live with your wives . . . (3:7)

Peter wasn't talking about simply taking up residence at the same address, sharing the same bed, eating at the same table, and paying off the same mortgage. The word *live* here suggests a "bond," a dwelling together that signifies the strength of the marriage union. Though some may consider marriage as an antiquated institution and others view it simply as a good tax break, God intends marriage to be an intimate union that illustrates the relationship of Christ and His bride, the church.

If a wife feels more comfortable baring her soul to a counselor than to her husband, her husband has dropped the ball. It is his job to provide an atmosphere of intimacy, honesty, and transparency. Peter exhorted men to love their wives and learn to search out the deepest needs and desires of their hearts.

Know Your Wife Deeply

Secondly, Peter described how a husband can foster intimacy with his wife.

> . . . live with your wives in an understanding way, as with someone weaker, since she is a woman . . . (3:7)

The Greek literally says, "Live with your wife according to knowledge." This does not mean that once a husband knows his wife's favorite colors, foods, and movies, he has finished the job. Peter's command refers to a lifetime of intentionality. It means husbands should pay more attention to their wives than to the remote control. It means they shouldn't simply offer monosyllabic answers to such questions as "How was your day?" or "Did you like your Bible study?" Like an archeologist searching for ancient treasure, a husband is instructed to carefully dust off his wife's dreams, discover her passions, and share her most difficult struggles.

It is important to note here that the term *weaker* refers only to a wife's smaller physical stature and lower level of brute strength. It does not imply inferiority of the wife or superiority of the husband in any way. On the contrary, the gentle, nurturing, feminine nature of the wife was created to complement the masculine nature of the husband. Husbands are commanded to love, protect, honor, respect, and cherish their wives as their own bodies (see Eph. 5:27–29).

Honor Your Wife Faithfully

Finally, and maybe most importantly, Peter commanded husbands to bestow honor upon their wives:

> . . . and show her honor as a fellow heir of the grace of life . . . (3:7)

The Greek word for *honor* was used to translate many Hebrew words in the Old Testament: *valuables, precious, honor, glory,* and *ransom.*[3] Peter carefully used this weighty word in three other key areas of his epistle (see 1 Peter 1:7; 1:19; 2:7). Wives are valuable, and Peter commanded husbands to grant them honor. Some men seem to view their wives more as maids than partners, more as nannies than mentors, and more as roommates than "fellow heirs of the grace of life." How might a man's actions toward his wife change if he realized he were married to royalty?

In order for a marriage to work, both partners must submit to the roles God ordained for them since Creation: wives, be submissive to your husbands; husbands, love your wives and meet their needs. If you start following the paths of "getting even" or "I'll show her" or "He needs to know this . . . ," you're doomed from the beginning.

Peter tucked the key to a successful marriage into the words of his letter. It's a simple plan, but it demands patience. It necessitates dying to self. It requires the Holy Spirit. And Peter summed it up in one word—*submission.*

 Living Insights

Why follow such counter-cultural advice? Does it come with a ninety-day, money-back guarantee? Does Peter promise it will thaw out your feelings, rekindle your romance, or jump-start your stalled-out marriage?

Read 1 Peter 3:7. Notice the last part of verse 7. What is the reason Peter cites for making submission and love a part of marriage?

_____

_____

_____

What does your spiritual life look like when your marriage is struggling?

_____

3. Gerhard Kittel and Gerhard Friedrich, eds., *The Theological Dictionary of the New Testament* (Grand Rapids, Mich.: William B. Eerdmans Publishing Company, 2000); accessed through the Logos Library System.

In 1 Peter 3:7, the word for *hinders* literally means "to cut into; [it] was used of impeding persons by breaking up the road, or by placing an obstacle sharply in the path: hence, metaphorically, of detaining a person unnecessarily."[4] If you, as a wife, are harboring bitterness, disrespect, or conditionality toward your husband, you've set up an unnecessary roadblock in your relationship with God.

Husbands, you may attend elder board meetings, lead men's retreats, or disciple younger men, but if you are also ignoring your wife, barely acknowledging her contributions, and assuming that by providing for her material needs you are loving her as Christ loved the church, then your spiritual life is being hindered.

Take a moment to evaluate your role. Think of a practical, realistic, and immediate way to submit to and love your spouse this week.

Wives, how can you change your attitude, actions, or attention?

_____

_____

_____

_____

_____

Husbands, how can you live intimately, know deeply, and honor your wife faithfully?

_____

_____

_____

_____

_____

4. W. E. Vine, *Vine's Expository Dictionary of Old and New Testament Words* (Grand Rapids, Mich.: Baker Book House Co., Fleming H. Revell, 1981); accessed through the Logos Library System.

 *Small Group Insights*

Marriages, both Christian and non-Christian, are floundering in our society. Unfortunately, many spouses are victims of "friendly fire"—attack from their partners. Insensitive comments fall like live hand grenades. Spouses meet confrontation with a bunker mentality. Instead of striving for victory, they find themselves hiding from or battling against each other. Our society helps little by publicizing broken marriages and ignoring those that succeed.

In your small group, take turns describing a marriage you admire. It could be your parents', grandparents', family friends', or a neighbor's. It should be one you have had time to examine. What made this marriage stand out? Share some qualities of a good marriage that you glean from the group's responses.

Then, discuss the following questions. You may wish to divide into smaller groups.

1. If you could improve one area in your marriage, what would it be?

2. In light of your study today, what is one practical way you can change your actions toward your spouse?

Chapter 5

NEW HOPE
TO REAL-WORLD BELIEVERS
1 Peter 4:1–11

Hollywood stereotypes Christians as "the religious right," "fundamentalist," "stuck in the mud," and "intolerant." Unfortunately, our society is critical of born-again believers, their stance, and their convictions. But this criticism is nothing new for Christians.

Throughout his first epistle, Peter provides new hope to believers who are facing difficult circumstances. For the early believers, injustice, unfairness, struggles, and even persecution were all active members of the "welcoming committee." Christians in first-century Rome were truly "aliens and strangers" living in an antagonistic world (Heb. 11:13 NIV).

Usually "aliens" want to remain anonymous. Communities stigmatize strangers. Yet Christ commanded us to "go into all the world and preach the gospel to all creation" (Mark 16:15). He commanded us to be "salt" and "light" (see Matt. 5:13–14). How can the alien win over a suspicious society? How can the light penetrate the darkness?

In chapter 4 of 1 Peter, we find the surprising answer.

Exhortation to Believers

Peter began chapter 4 with a three-letter Greek word. Little words in Greek often have big meanings. Translated as "therefore," this term should prompt the reader to ask, "What is it *there for?*" Peter drew his conclusion from the previous thought presented in 3:18 and 22:

> For Christ also died for sins once for all, the just for the unjust, so that He might bring us to God, having been put to death in the flesh, but made alive in the spirit . . . who is at the right hand of God, having gone into heaven, after angels and authorities and powers had been subjected to Him.

Peter swept through one of the most thought-provoking subjects in all of theology — the incarnation. God became flesh in the person of Christ, who was perfectly human and perfect deity. He came to earth to die so that we might live. After His resurrection, He ascended to heaven, to the right hand of the Father. He left, but He sent the Holy Spirit to dwell in the hearts of believers, to comfort and guide them. In light of these overwhelming truths, Peter exhorted believers to action:

> Therefore, since Christ has suffered in the flesh, arm yourselves also with the same purpose. (1 Peter 4:1a)

Just as Christ suffered physically, so too his followers would be subjected to various hardships. *Arm* is a military word used in the New Testament to refer to a soldier putting on armor (see Eph. 6:13). Using the same kind of determination and care, believers are to equip themselves with the attitude of Christ — "an unswerving resolve to do God's will."[1] Commentator Kenneth Wuest provides an apt illustration of this unique metaphor:

> [Peter] exhorts the saints to arm themselves with the same mind that Christ had regarding unjust punishment. . . . The Greek word translated "arm yourselves" was used of a Greek soldier putting on his armor and taking his weapons. The noun of the same root was used of a heavy-armed footsoldier who carried a pike and a large shield. . . . The Christian needs the heaviest armor he can get to withstand the attacks of the enemy of his soul.[2]

We are soldiers, not tourists simply passing through life to observe and take pictures. The goal of the Christian life is not just to go to church, but to make a difference in a dark world.

Transformation of the Believer

The Lord has not left us without encouragement for our battle:

> . . . because he who has suffered in the flesh has ceased from sin, so as to live the rest of the time in

---

1. John F. Walvoord and Roy B. Zuck, eds., *The Bible Knowledge Commentary* (Wheaton, Ill.: Scripture Press Publications Inc., 1983, 1985); accessed through the Logos Library System.

2. Kenneth Wuest, *First Peter: In the Greek New Testament*, as quoted by Ken Gire in the Bible study guide *Hope in Hurtful Times*, from the Bible-teaching ministry of Charles R. Swindoll (Anaheim, Calif.: Insight for Living, 1990), p. 87.

the flesh no longer for the lusts of men, but for the will of God. (1 Peter 4:1–2)

Peter lists three benefits for those who are "in Christ." First, sin no longer has mastery over the believer (v. 1b). Secondly, we can overcome the desires that rule the unbeliever (v. 2a). Thirdly, we have the opportunity to fulfill God's will (v. 2b). The apostle continues with a vivid picture of a life void of Christ:

> For the time already past is sufficient for you to have carried out the desire of the Gentiles, having pursued a course of sensuality, lusts, drunkenness, carousing, drinking parties and abominable idolatries. (1 Peter 4:3)

Some of you reading this were born on a Saturday and squirming in the pew the next day at church. For you, the church has provided a hedge of protection throughout your life. You began your relationship with Christ early and have followed Him fervently. Consider yourself blessed!

But for others, reading this verse takes you back to the scene of the crime. You remember the brief "highs" of pleasure followed by the long-lasting guilt, the stifling shame, and the abyss of purposelessness. Peter's list stirs faint images of your former life when, instead of hungering for God, you followed empty passions.

The word *sensuality* in this verse characterizes actions that bring disgust and shock public decency. The term *lusts* is not limited to sexual promiscuity, but includes any passionate desire that is out of control and therefore sinful. "Drunkenness, carousings, and drinking parties" bring to mind the infamous Roman orgies. Though Peter was referring to pagan customs in the first century, he could have been peering through a window at modern times.

Such a wild, wanton life filled with selfish consumption can never satisfy the spiritual void in depraved hearts. It's like eating potato chips for Thanksgiving dinner instead of a lavish feast of succulent carved turkey, steaming mashed potatoes and gravy, tangy cranberry sauce, and sweet, spicy pumpkin pie. C. S. Lewis said:

> It would seem that Our Lord finds our desires not too strong, but too weak. We are half-hearted creatures, fooling about with drink and sex and ambition when infinite joy is offered us, like an ignorant child

who wants to go on making mud pies in a slum because he cannot imagine what is meant by the offer of a holiday at the sea. We are far too easily pleased.[3]

We settle for so much less than what God wants for us. Yet God mercifully still loves us, saves us from our sin, and transforms our lives.

Reaction of the World

Though Heaven rejoices with each salvation, the lost world responds with one of two emotions. Peter described the first this way:

> In all this, they are surprised that you do not run with them into the same excesses of dissipation . . .
> (1 Peter 4:4)

In every age, from the first century to the twenty-first century, when a person turns from worldly pleasures to follow Christ, people will be "surprised." The New Living Translation renders this verse: "Of course, your former friends are very surprised when you no longer join them in the wicked things they do."

Peter contends that shock and confusion concerning a believer's conversion can quickly turn into something more dangerous:

> . . . and they malign you. (1 Peter 4:4b)

A Christian's light threatens the crowd who still craves to "run with . . . the same excess of dissipation (v. 4)." A new life in Christ exposes darkened hearts. Jesus stated, "The light from heaven came into the world, but they loved the darkness more than the light, for their actions were evil. They hate the light because they want to sin in the darkness" (John 3:19–20 NLT).

The Fifth Special Forces Group, a unit of the United States Army, arrived in Somalia in 1992 to provide protection for a humanitarian mission. Though under the banner of peace, they meticulously armed themselves daily because hostile warlords ravaged the surrounding regions. Some of the people welcomed the liberators; others met them with weapons. The destitute treated them like heroes; the defiant treated them like enemies. Eventually, on one fateful raid, nineteen American soldiers died on the streets of

---

3. C. S. Lewis, from a sermon entitled "The Weight of Glory," as quoted by John Piper in *Desiring God* (Sisters, Ore.: Questar Publishers Inc., Multnomah Books, 1996), p. 17.

Mogadishu. They died carrying out a mission and fulfilling the group's unique motto: "Liberate the Oppressed."

In the same way, Jesus sent us to bring a message of liberation to those oppressed by sin's stranglehold. When you become a believer in Christ, some people will be pleasantly surprised by your transformation, and your offer of new life will be met with open arms. Others' shock may turn into chagrin or malice. Though Christians may be hounded by hostility from others, Peter assured us that those people "shall give an account to Him who is ready to judge the living and the dead" (4:5). Their actions will not go unnoticed by the sovereign Lord.

Furthermore, Peter maintained that our struggles will not last forever.

> The end of all things is near . . . (1 Peter 4:7a)

Our time is short. And because of that, our mission is to invade our communities with His grace. In a world that regards believers with surprise or repugnance, what will motivate others to approach the Light? Peter introduced four commands to guide the believer who is surrounded by a disbelieving world.

Four Commands on How to Shock a Suspicious Society

Use Good Judgment and Stay Calm in a Spirit of Prayer

Peter lived under two stressful realities: (1) Christ could return at any moment and (2) a Christian's life could be snuffed out in an instant at the whim of a fickle dictator like Nero. In light of this, one might expect Peter to act hurried, harried, and hyper. Instead, he issues a command that confounds the world's wisdom:

> . . . therefore, be of sound judgment and sober spirit for the purpose of prayer. (1 Peter 4:7b)

Peter expounded on this command later in his epistle by exhorting believers to "[cast] all your anxiety on Him, because He cares for you. Be of sober spirit, be on the alert" (5:7–8). Be wary of the world, but not worried. Be remorseful through sufferings, but not resigned. In persecutions, Christians persevere. In trials, believers triumph. When pressed, saints pray, because Christians know who is ultimately in control.

Stay Fervent in Love

Peter's second command encourages believers to focus on love:

Above all, keep fervent in your love for one another, because love covers a multitude of sins. (4:8)

The Greek reads "keep love constant," or be "strained"[4] in your love. It pictures "the taut muscles of an athlete who strains to win a race."[5] This is how Christians should love each other — with passion and perseverance. Why? Peter's words paraphrase Proverbs 10:12: "Hatred stirs up strife, but love covers all sins" (NKJV).

Think of someone who needs your love, not your judgment. He or she may have blown it in the past, but repented and returned. Now it's your turn to leave grudges to the world and open your arms to your friend with a forgiving embrace. By doing so, you will demonstrate the love of Christ.

As Jesus prepared His disciples for His departure, He left them with this powerful statement: "Your love for one another will prove to the world that you are my disciples" (John 13:35 NLT). The world will know you are a Christian by your love. That love should also spill over to your family, your friends, your colleagues, and your neighborhood. Let it filter through those who have never felt the unconditional, *agape* love of Christ.

Be Hospitable

Be hospitable to one another without complaint. (1 Peter 4:9)

The term *hospitable* comes from combining two Greek words meaning "love" and "stranger." *Hospitality* literally means "showing love to strangers." Hospitality takes time, effort, and money, and often it requires an invasion of privacy. However, it also offers many rewards. Here Peter commands followers of Christ to exercise such love among each other without complaint.

How's your hospitality? Is your schedule so busy that you rarely seek out your neighbors except to borrow a weedeater or a cup of

---

4. Walter Bauer, F. Wilbur Gingrich, and Frederick W. Danker, eds., *A Greek-English Lexicon of the New Testament and Other Early Christian Literature* (Chicago, Ill.: University of Chicago Press, 1979); accessed through the Logos Library System.

5. Walvoord and Zuck, *The Bible Knowledge Commentary*; accessed through the Logos Library System.

flour? When was the last time you entertained the downcast, depressed, or depraved? Is your house a lighted inn on the road of loneliness? Your hospitality will cause the world to wonder what motivates such kindness. Reach out. Provide a place for others to seek refuge. Have a heart. Seek to extend God's love, comfort, and support to others.

Keep Serving One Another

As each one has received a special gift, employ it in serving one another as good stewards of the manifold grace of God. (1 Peter 4:10)

Peter, a fisherman, kept his commands simple, practical, and to the point. He concluded plainly that all of us have been given gifts and we are expected to use them. The early church did not have the benefit of personality testing, spiritual gift inventories, or Bible conferences. So Peter gave the believers of that day some guidelines concerning spiritual gifts:

Whoever speaks, is to do so as one who is speaking the utterances of God; whoever serves is to do so as one who is serving by the strength which God supplies. (4:10–11a)

Peter lumped spiritual gifts into two overall categories: *speaking* and *serving*.[6] In addition, He addressed how the believer is to exercise his or her gift: *willingly* and *dependently*. Stop wondering if you are talented enough, polished enough, or good enough to serve in the church. The body of Christ is dependent upon each member's unique gifts and each member's willing participation (see 1 Cor. 12). Peter illustrates that spiritual gifts should only be exercised using the Lord's strength. That way, He alone is glorified. If someone seeks his or her own glory, then he or she supplants the overall goal of Peter's exhortations and fails to edify the body of Christ.

Goal—That God May Be Glorified

Ultimately our actions will lead to one goal—that the world may see Christ in us.

6. For a more complete listing of the spiritual gifts referred to in Scripture, see Romans 12:1–8; 1 Corinthians 12; Ephesians 4:11–13; and 1 Peter 4:10–11.

. . . so that in all things God may be glorified
through Jesus Christ, to whom belongs the glory and
dominion forever and ever. Amen. (1 Peter 4:11b)

When we portray a calm spirit, fervent love, hospitable lives,
and service to one another, we will shock the world! We will be a
fork in the road of other people's lives, showing them a better path.
Some may malign us for being so counter-cultural. But others may
be so surprised at our lifestyle that they will be drawn to the source
of such incomprehensible grace — the almighty God.

 Living Insights

The early church acted upon Peter's command to tangibly and
sacrificially love one another. One outsider observed: "It is incred-
ible to see the ardor with which the people of that religion [Chris-
tianity] help each other in their wants. They spare nothing. Their
first legislator [Christ] has put into their heads that they are all
brethren."[7]

Take a moment to read Acts 2:37–47. What were some attributes of the early church?

_____

_____

_____

_____

Think about your church. From the list you gathered above, in
what areas does your church excel, and in what areas does your
church need improvement?

_____

_____

_____

_____

7. Philip Schaff, *History of the Christian Church* (Oak Harbor, Wash.: Logos Research Systems,
Inc., 1997); accessed through the Logos Library System.

In what tangible ways can you personally emulate the early church as described in Acts? In the space below, write out a covenant with God, listing steps you can take to express your love for others in a practical way.

_____

_____

_____

_____

_____

_____

_____

_____

_____

_____

_____

_____

Small Group Insights

For three years, Jesus' teaching reverberated through the tiny region known as Palestine. His preaching stymied authorities. Religious leaders stumbled over his words. He stumped even the greatest of men. The people marveled that He "spoke as one with authority" (Mark 1:22). But Jesus' words were always accompanied by His works. His truth was authenticated by proof. Jesus not only painted the kingdom of God in the minds of the multitudes, He let them see, hear, smell, taste, and touch it. He let them *experience* it.

As a group, follow the footsteps of Jesus using the chart provided on the next page. Divide up into smaller groups and complete it, using the examples provided. Split up the verses and report back after ten or fifteen minutes. As a group, discuss Jesus' ministry.

VERSES	AUDIENCE	ACTION(S)
Mark 2:1–12	Multitudes in Capernaum; paralytic and friends	Forgiveness, healing of the paralytic
Mark 5:1–20		
Mark 5:25–43		
Mark 6:33–44		
Mark 7:24–37		
Mark 8:1–10		
Mark 10:13–16		

Read Mark 10:44–45. As you look over the chart, explain specifically how Jesus served those who had experienced hurts or unmet needs in the following areas:

- Spiritual

- Intellectual

- Physical

- Emotional

- Racial

- Cultural

Though His preaching stunned the crowds, it was Jesus' actions that shocked the world. Think about the last time your church tangibly reached out to the community. How can your small group or church seek to meet the needs of your congregation or community? Here are some examples: plan a work day or building project; hold a fundraiser to help your community; volunteer at a soup kitchen; organize a small group mission trip. List your ideas in the space below. Be creative! The Lord will honor your willing hearts.

_____

_____

_____

_____

_____

_____

_____

Jesus said in the Sermon on the Mount, "Let your light shine before men in such a way that they may see your good works, and glorify your Father who is in Heaven" (Matt. 5:16). When we glorify God, we shine brightly before others. Remember: They don't care how much you know until they know how much you care.

Chapter 6

NEW HOPE
AT YOUR CHURCH
1 Peter 5:1–7

Peter often came across like a biblical "bull in a china shop." This rugged fisherman was tender at times, but at others, he threw etiquette out the window and let angry words fly. His actions and emotions boiled over, leaving hearts in broken pieces. Though Jesus called Peter from netting fish in the seas of Galilee to catching men on the shores of Galilee, Simon's words and phrases still reflected his background as a rough, little-educated fisherman.

But something happened to Peter after Jesus' resurrection. God used Peter's powerful personality, inner strength, and fortitude to lead the church's first great revival on the day of Pentecost. Afterwards, his demeanor began to change to suit his continuing ministry. The burly fisherman became a gentle shepherd.

Shepherd—what an apt metaphor for a leader. Jesus said of Himself, "I am the good shepherd, and I know My own and My own know Me" (John 10:14). In a day when other leaders used any means necessary to get ahead, Jesus humbly knelt, like the lowliest of servants, to wash His disciples' feet. He modeled true leadership through service. And no image captures the self-sacrifice, the patience, and the loneliness of leadership better than that of a shepherd leading his sheep.

Perhaps you are serving as a shepherd to sheep of your own. Your sheep may be a congregation, a family, a discipleship group, or a nursery full of rambunctious two-year-olds. Some of your greatest frustrations may come when you encounter bleating, wayward, struggling lambs. How can you lead without letting your frustration and emotions boil over? How can you be effective in helping people with their greatest need of all—finding spiritual maturity? What does a shepherd look like today?

In the previous chapters, Peter's apt advice filled our hearts with new hope to face some of life's greatest trials. And once again we sit at his feet and take notes as he paints the portrait of a shepherd.

Two Aspects of a Good Elder

> Therefore, I exhort the elders among you, as your fellow elder and witness of the sufferings of Christ, and a partaker also of the glory that is to be revealed . . . (1 Peter 5:1)

Peter began by stripping away any pride of position. Notice that he did not pull rank with other believers. He could have easily backed up his command with an appeal to his apostleship. In fact, though he addressed himself as "an apostle of Jesus Christ" in 1 Peter 1:1, he identified himself here as a "fellow elder." Peter sidled up to the reader and said, "I'm one of you. I know your struggle."

The word *partaker* has the sense of "partner, associate, comrade, [and] companion."[1] Here, a disciple from Jesus' inner circle locked arms with those he led. Look how far Peter had come! Some of the Gospel accounts portray Peter as a gruff fisherman intent on being second-in-command to Jesus. But here we see a true and tender leader with a servant's heart. Two aspects of leadership are evident in his life.

Pride Must Be Absent

Pride creates a minefield in the midst of ministry. Many church leaders are gifted. But too often they begin to believe their press reports, take tacit credit for their success, and put themselves in the place of God. Those who do so risk the chastisement of a jealous God. J. Oswald Sanders wrote this in his masterful book on leadership:

> Nothing is more distasteful to God than self-conceit. This first and fundamental sin in essence aims at enthroning self at the expense of God. . . . Pride is a sin of whose presence its victim is least conscious. . . . If we are honest, when we measure ourselves by the life of our Lord who humbled Himself even to death on a cross, we cannot but be overwhelmed with the tawdriness and shabbiness, and even the vileness, of our hearts.[2]

1. James Strong, *Enhanced Strong's Lexicon*, (Ontario, Canada: Woodside Bible Fellowship, 1996); accessed through the Logos Library System.

2. J. Oswald Sanders, *Spiritual Leadership*, as quoted by Charles R. Swindoll in *The Tale of the Tardy Oxcart and 1,501 Other Stories* (Nashville, Tenn.: Word Publishing, 1998), p. 468.

Peter contended that we are all "fellow elders." We may have differing gifts, skills, or charisma, but there is only one Giver and only one who receives glory. The minute we take credit, we discredit the work of our heavenly Father.

The Heart of a Shepherd Must Be Present

> Therefore, I exhort the elders among you . . . shepherd the flock of God among you . . . (1 Peter 5:1–2a)

If you lead or serve anyone in the church, replace your title of deacon, elder, Sunday school teacher, or discipleship leader with "shepherd." Peter wrote to you—all those who struggle with sheep, fend off danger, and sit lonely upon the hill.

The command to shepherd, or be like a shepherd, is the same one Jesus gave to Peter in John 21:16. Shepherding involved constant protection, care, and attention. The effectiveness of a good shepherd was not measured by his style or his flair with the staff, but rather by the shepherd's familiarity with the sheep and their response to him:

> Living and working with sheep in isolation leads to a close relationship between shepherd and sheep. The shepherds know their sheep so well that they respond to them instantly. The shepherd has a name for each sheep, the significance being that the name says something about the individual sheep's character or mannerisms.[3]

Notice to whom the flock belongs: "the flock *of* God among you." In biblical times, the sheep under a shepherd's care usually belonged to someone else. In fact, often a village employed a shepherd to care for everyone's sheep.[4] Peter makes it clear who possesses ownership of the people in our care. We are merely "under-shepherds" of the Chief Shepherd, who, in His grace, has allowed us to lead His sheep (1 Peter 5:4). Our love for Christ motivates our concern for His flock.

---

3. Ralph Gower, *The New Manners and Customs of Bible Times* (Chicago, Ill.: Moody Press, 1987), p. 140.

4. Gower, *The New Manners and Customs of Bible Times*, p. 133.

Three Essential Attitudes

Peter next shared three essential attitudes of a leader. His words tell us first how *not* to act and then how to effectively lead the people in our care.

An Attitude of Willingness

> . . . exercising oversight not under compulsion, but voluntarily, according to the will of God . . . (5:2b)

Peter did not use the pulpit to manipulate people to volunteer for jobs for which they had not been gifted. He recognized that leadership is a higher calling. Likewise, the apostle James warns that few should seek to be teachers, for God judges them more severely (James 3:1). Peter seeks a volunteer army to further God's kingdom; He's recruiting men and women who know they will often be overworked and underpaid. He seeks servants who shepherd out of a desire to obey and honor God, not a need for accolades.

The rewards will be few and, at times, the sacrifice great. The great preacher Charles Haddon Spurgeon wrote in *Lectures to My Students*:

> Fits of depression come over most of us. Usually cheerful as we may be, we must at intervals be cast down. The strong are not always vigorous, the wise not always ready, the brave not always courageous, and the joyous not always happy. There may be here and there men of iron . . . but surely the rust frets even these.[5]

What revealing words! As a volunteer, you will need times of refreshment and exhortation. Even Jesus spent time in solitude on a mountaintop to be with His Father and pray. God is the source of our refreshment and inspiration. You can only give what first has been given to you. Serve God willingly, but allow Him to refresh you in the midst of your service.

An Attitude of Eagerness

> . . . and not for sordid gain, but with eagerness . . . (1 Peter 5:2c)

---

5. Charles Haddon Spurgeon, *Lectures to My Students*, as quoted by Charles R. Swindoll in *The Tale of the Tardy Oxcart and 1,501 Other Stories* (Nashville, Tenn.: Word Publishing, 1998), p. 159.

It seems every year we hear of a televangelist or a prominent church leader involved in some financial scandal. Not only should a shepherd lead with willingness, but he or she should also avoid focusing on personal profit. While money itself is not sinful, the Bible says that the love of money is the root of all sorts of evil (see 1 Tim. 6:10). Many a shepherd loses track of the sheep when he or she focuses on wealth.

Peter suggests that a leader's motive should be one of "eagerness." Peter exhorts leaders to have a zeal for their charges, the sheep. Your sheep may question your direction, your style, or your purpose, but you as the shepherd are called to goad them earnestly to places beyond their frustrations.

An Attitude of Meekness

> . . . nor yet as lording it over those allotted to your charge, but proving to be examples to the flock. (1 Peter 5:3)

Peter was there when two impetuous disciples asked the question all the other disciples had on their minds: "Grant that we may sit, one on Your right and one on Your left, in Your glory." (Mark 10:37) The disciples, oblivious of Christ's purpose on earth, jockeyed for future positions of leadership and glory. Jesus' response stymied their pride and stuck with Peter long into his ministry:

> "You know that those who are recognized as rulers of the Gentiles lord it over them; and their great men exercise authority over them. But it is not this way among you, but whoever wishes to become great among you shall be your servant; and whoever wishes to be first among you shall be slave of all." (Mark 10:42–45)

"Lording it over" carries with it the idea of dominance, oppression, and demands. The world may practice this as a form of leadership, but in contrast, a shepherd models humility, sacrifice, and meekness. The world says, "Look out for yourself." Peter said, "Look out for your sheep."

The Reward

Peter desired those who tend the flocks of God to know that their efforts are not in vain.

And when the Chief Shepherd appears, you will
receive the unfading crown of glory. (1 Peter 5:4)

The Chief Shepherd will come to reward the under-shepherds!
Though the world may not recognize your efforts, though people
in your church may not recognize the lonely hours you have spent
on the hill taking care of them, the Good Shepherd sees. He knows.
The glories of this world tarnish quickly, but the reward Jesus gives
shines for eternity.

A Final Exhortation

First Peter closes with a reminder that leaders in the church
should constantly check their motives:

> You younger men, likewise, be subject to your elders;
> and all of you, clothe yourselves with humility to-
> ward one another, for God is opposed to the proud,
> but gives grace to the humble. (5:5)

The book of 1 Peter establishes a hierarchy in the church that
contradicts the world's model. Today our culture rewards youth and
puts celebrities on pedestals. The greater someone's beauty and
fame, the more influential they are perceived to be. We value youth,
strength, and vivaciousness; the older generation is viewed as antiquated, stuck in the mud, and irrelevant. But Peter challenged
this paradigm. He asked the young to give preference to their elders,
and not vice versa.

Secondly, Peter commanded all of us to put on new clothes:
"Clothe yourself with humility." Don the cloak of a servant. Put
on the garment of deference. Look out more for the interests of
others than your own. If you are a shepherd for the fame, for the
glory, for personal fanfare, you're in the wrong business. Peter
warned that God stiff-arms the proud. God knows your motives.
God's hand can bestow blessing or dole out discipline. Peter exhorted us to choose blessing:

> Therefore humble yourselves under the mighty hand
> of God, that He may exalt you at the proper time,
> casting all your anxiety on Him, because He cares
> for you. (5:6–7)

Leadership is fraught with snares and struggles. Peter did not
deny the frustration and pain often associated with the shepherd's

job of caring for people. Rather, he offered new hope for the struggle by encouraging a spirit of willing humility. Take his words to heart. Lead the flock of God with the heart of the Great Shepherd.

 Living Insights

Leadership seminars stop at every major city. Self-help books pack the shelves at every bookstore. Self-appointed success gurus ply their trade on infomercials and radio programs. Everywhere you turn, someone is pontificating on managing success and successful managing. But there are few maxims or methods that can match the philosophy of leadership pictured in the Twenty-Third Psalm. Take a moment to meditate on Eugene Peterson's rendering of the words in contemporary language:

Psalm 23

God, my shepherd!
> I don't need a thing.
You have bedded me down in lush meadows,
> you find me quiet pools to drink from.
True to your word,
> you let me catch my breath
> and send me in the right direction.

Even when the way goes through
> Death Valley,
I'm not afraid
> when you walk at my side.
Your trusty shepherd's crook
> makes me feel secure.

You serve me a six-course dinner
> right in front of my enemies.
You revive my drooping head;
> my cup brims with blessing.

Your beauty and love chase after me
> every day of my life.
I'm back home in the house of God
> for the rest of my life.[6] (THE MESSAGE)

6. Eugene H. Peterson, *The Message: The New Testament, Psalms and Proverbs* (Colorado Springs, Colo.: Navpress, 1995).

Now look back through this portrait of the Good Shepherd and notice every brushstroke regarding leadership. Pick out a few themes that impact you the most and write them down.

_____

_____

_____

Choose one theme that you could develop in your own ministry. How can you better shepherd those God has entrusted to you? Whether it be your discipleship group, congregation, or kids, seek to implement the practiced and proven methods outlined in this comforting psalm.

_____

_____

_____

Small Group Insights

When Moses was preparing to pass the torch to Joshua, Yahweh commanded Moses to *encourage* Joshua in light of the monumental task (Deut. 1:38). What wise counsel! Leaders often do thankless jobs and seek no praise. However, timely encouragement can do wonders to reenergize and refresh shepherds.

Read Hebrews 3:13 and 10:25. What is the major theme of these two verses?

_____

_____

_____

Can you think of some varying leadership styles presented in Scripture? Break up into groups and come up with as many leaders as you can and list their prominent attributes.

_____

_____

_____

_____

_____

_____

Think of some leaders who have impacted your life—past and present. They might be pastors, small group leaders, coaches, city officials, youth leaders, coworkers, parents, relatives, or friends. What made these people and their leadership styles significant in your life?

_____

_____

_____

As a group, take some time to pray for the leaders who influence your lives.

Now, take some time to brainstorm an idea to tangibly honor and encourage those leaders. Here are a few suggestions:

Leadership Oscar Night—Give out awards recognizing the leadership style of pastors or lay leaders in your congregation: a Stephen Award for a servant leader; a Barnabas Award for a great encourager; an Elijah Award for a leader with strong convictions in a wayward society. Make it memorable time that honors God for His provision of gifted shepherds in your lives.

Pastor Date Night—Honor your pastor(s) by providing a babysitter for his kids and taking him out with your small group for a special dinner. Present him with a plaque signifying years of dedicated service to your community. Or, offer to babysit one night a month so your pastor and his wife can have their own "date night."

Anonymous Letters—Each month, have someone in your group write an encouraging, anonymous letter to a leader (or leaders) in your church. At the end of the year, these leaders will have at least twelve reminders of how God has specifically used them in the ministry.

BOOKS FOR
PROBING FURTHER

Our journey through the book of 1 Peter has come to an end. Though your hardships in this world may never cease, we pray this study has served as a beacon to guide you to calmer waters. Our hope is that Christ will bless you with new hope in the midst of even your most severe trials. We trust this book has helped you with practical, real-life application of the powerful and relevant Word of God.

To provide you with the opportunity to explore these topics more deeply, we wish to recommend the following books. As you continue your travels through the Christian life, we hope these books will make your road smoother and your journey more refreshing.

Dobson, James. *Love for a Lifetime: Building a Marriage That Will Go the Distance*. Sisters, Ore.: Multnomah Publications Inc., 2001.

Lewis, C. S. *The Problem of Pain*. San Francisco, Calif.: Harper Row, 2001.

Lewis, Robert, and William Hendricks. *Rocking the Roles: Building a Win-Win Marriage*. Colorado Springs, Colo.: Navpress, 1991.

Lucado, Max. *Traveling Light: Releasing Burdens You Were Never Intended to Bear*. Dallas, Tex.: Word Publishing, 2001.

Nouwen, Henri. *Turn My Mourning into Dancing: Finding Hope in Hard Times*. Dallas, Tex.: Word Publishing, 2001.

Swindoll, Charles R. *Hope Again*. Dallas, Tex.: Word Publishing, 1996.

———. *Laugh Again*. Dallas, Tex.: Word Publishing, 1995.

Wiersbe, Warren. *Be Hopeful*. Wheaton, Ill.: Victor Books, 1982.

Yancey, Philip. *Where Is God When It Hurts?* Grand Rapids, Mich.: Zondervan, 1977.

Some of the books listed may be out of print and available only through a library. For those currently available, please contact your local Christian bookstore. Books by Charles R. Swindoll may be obtained through the Insight for Living Resource Center, as well as many books by other authors. Just call the IFL office that serves you.

Insight for Living also has Bible study guides available on many books of the Bible as well as on a variety of topics, Bible characters, and contemporary issues. For more information, see the ordering instructions that follow and contact the office that serves you.

NOTES

NOTES

NOTES

NOTES

ORDERING INFORMATION

NEW HOPE FOR LIFE'S CHALLENGES

If you would like to order additional Bible study guides, purchase the audiocassette series that accompanies this guide, or request our product catalogs, please contact the office that serves you.

United States and International locations:
Insight for Living
Post Office Box 269000
Plano, TX 75026-9000

1-800-772-8888, 24 hours a day, seven days a week (U.S. contacts) International constituents may contact the U.S. office through mail queries.

Canada:
Insight for Living Ministries
Post Office Box 2510
Vancouver, BC V6B 3W7

1-800-663-7639, 24 hours a day, seven days a week
insight.canada@insight.org

Australia:
Insight for Living, Inc.
20 Albert Street
Blackburn, VIC 3130, Australia

Toll-free 1800 772 888 or (03) 9877-4277, 9:00 A.M. to 5:00 P.M., Monday to Friday
insight.aus@insight.org

Internet:
www.insight.org

Bible Study Guide Subscription Program

Bible study guide subscriptions are available. Please call or write the office nearest you to find out how you can receive our Bible study guides on a regular basis.